ISBN:

IMPARTING BEFORE DEPARTING

ACKNOWLEDGMENTS

All glory and adoration be to the ancient well that never runs dry; Yahweh is His name. Only you hath made my hand like the pen of a ready writer

The Gospel Faith Mission International (GOFAMINT) is my cave of Adullam and i am eternally grateful to identify with her. Words will not be enough to appreciate my spiritual father; Rev. (Dr.) Taylor Karl (*Setman of Treasure youth Gathering*), Dr. Dolly (*Psychiatric Consultant*), Pastor Shola Alabi (*Living Spring Network*) for sharing inspiring thoughts borne out of their dealings and consistent walk with God in this book. All TYG ministers all duely acknowledged.

Unreserved celebration to Daddy and Mummy & my siblings for both raising me in the way of the lord and creating a homely atmosphere to be the best I can be. A big thank you to pastor Bright Moses who wrote the foreword of this book, I still glean from your wisdom hitherto. I celebrate Pastor Marvelous input behind the scene, Sis. Oyindamola and Bro. Tunde massive effort to ensure this great project is successful will not go unnoticed. I owe you all more than I can ever repay.

TABLE OF CONTENTS

FOREWORD

Any existence on this planet Earth without indelible marks is a colossal waste. I likened such life to a life of Solomon Grundy whose life's summary turned to Nursery rhyme. *Solomon Grundy, Born on a Monday, Chritened on Tuesday, married on Wednesday, took I'll on Thursday, grew worst on Friday, died on Saturday, buried on Sunday. That was the end of Solomon Grundy.*

There has never been a record of what he achieved during his life time. Your generation must know you or remember you for something. Jesus Christ who is our role model spent about three years in ministry before this departure, but the impacts of that three years can't be quantified by anything because it lasts till eternity. He said "it is finished" on the cross (John 19:30), which means "He had emptied and delivered what He was sent to do in life". Beloved, God expects all-round impacts from you. It could be impact through your career, academics, ministry etc. A man spent about three years in earth and the effects of His living humanity can't recover from it till eternity. He lived a life of impact that heaven and Earth could testify to it.

Methuselah spent many years without a single impact recorded for him but Solomon with the little years he spent his wisdom lasts forever. *That is why the longevity of Methuselah cannot be compared with sagacity of Solomon*. And what made the difference was his impacts. It is not how far!. May you not exist but live! There is difference between existing and living. You exists to cumber the environment but you live to impact the environment. That is why many are existing, but few are living. I am trusting the grace of God over this young dynamic man of God that this annual publication will not only inspire you but will stand as a block-booster to discover the intrinsic treasures to impact your world.

Pastor Bright Moses

(GOFAMINT, Ipetu Ijesha)

IMPACTING BEFORE DEPARTING (IBD) EXPLAINED

Life is a trust and must be lived with intentionality and every sense of mission. Howbeit, there are two kinds of people in this world; *impact maker* and *impact watcher.* Although the sovereign God wired everyone with every potential and possibilities to identify with the first cadre. However, the narrative changes when we landed in time as many charted a course God never ordained for them owning to ignorance, wrong ideologies, refusal to partner with life principle etc. What a pain it is to watch people make impact and never numbered among them and much more painful to appear in Zion with nothing to show for the life you have been trusted with.

IBD is an annual publication inspired at stirring the heart of men up that we are created for more, impacting winning spirit by contending against mediocrity, provoking God's given abilities and potentials locked up on our inside and stimulating the mindset of men towards impact within the limited timeframe we have on earth. It is launched on June 2 of every year which apparently is the birthday of the visioneer. Don't settle for less you carry in you a DNA of eternal relevance. Learn what it takes to live an enviable life on earth from the mysteries of men and women of proven results and also etch your name in the sand of time even when you are long gone. Happy reading

David, of course, having completed the work God set out for him, has been in grave, dust and ashes, a long time now. [MSB]

Acts 13:36

SOUND THE ALARM

Tell anyone who is on a mission to happen to get God early in life;

Tell anyone who is intentional about greatness not to despise the days of little;

Tell anyone who want to perpetually stand before men to master the mystery of sitting to learn firsthand,

Tell anyone who long to impact before departing to understand the mystery of the errand of life;

Tell anyone who is earnestly contending for the crown to pay the price lawfully;

Tell anyone who is striving for mastery in every department of life to be temperate in all things,

Tell anyone who is interested in going far to stand on the shoulder of those who have gone on before,

Tell anyone who desires their names to be etched in the sand of time to follow them who through faith has obtained the promises;

Tell anyone who really desire lasting result to master the process not the product,

Tell anyone who yearns for fulfillments in life and destiny to find purpose and stay true to their callings;

Tell anyone who desire to man their gates in destiny to remain humble and lowly in heart regardless of divine lifting,

Tell anyone who looks forward to being a great leader to first become a faithful servant,

Tell anyone who want to strike a cord in life to thoroughly master godliness, dilligence, tenacity, contentment and consistency,

Tell anyone journey through life not to spend the transport fare as it will take longer time to arrive at destination; if they ever arrive at all.

Bill C. Newman

CHAPTER ONE

THE ERRAND OF LIFE

Without mincing words, it is obvious and convincing beyond reasonable doubt that many are yet to apprehend the true definition of life by reason of way and manner they live their lives daily. In my short little life I have perpetually seen it written all over some folks their misconception about life which is evidence in their misplaced priorities, major in minor and vice versa, weight of character deficient, dishonor to principle of life etc. however, it is practically impossible to make most of life if we do not fully grasp its essence and purpose.

"If the purpose of a thing is not known abuse is inevitable."

Anonymous

What Life is Not!

- **Massive Material Possession**

"And he said unto them, Take heed, and beware of coveteousness; for a man's life consisteth not in the abundance of the things he posseseth." Luke 12:15

We have all been bewitched to think life is all about materialism and abundance of possession and as a result everyone is on a rat race to be a custodian of these mundane things. Living in ultra-modern edifice, flaunting the latest automobile, making the forbes' list and many more is our definition of life at its peak whereas this is nothing but a misconception. This is not in any way downplaying the significance of economic capacity and material possession. However, the errand of life is higher than things that can be seen and touch. Regrettably, an average young men and women is under pressure to meet up with societal demand, make end meet, remain relevant in the 21st century ecosystem and as a result have been forced to do the unimaginable owning to this misinformation. In this hot pursuit, some have met with terrible disaster, many have been sent to early grave while the few alive have been sentenced to an eternal hellish life in their inordinate quest.

The sadder reality is our younger generation has now swallowed this cancerous information hook line and sinker. They are not sparing any effort to making sure they identify with money monguls of the land regardless of any consequences. They have a mindset that is terrible and their apathy for education is out of this world. At this juncture, if there is ever going to be a hope for our generation, we must intentionally begin to sound the alarm after the order of Christ that "a man's life consist not in the abundance of the things which he has".

- **Food and Raiment**

"The life is more than meat, and the body is more than raiment." Luke 12:23

Another undoing of our generation is the obsession of "what to eat" and "what to wear". You will be shocked as to the extent people can go all in the name of eating and clothing. I place so much value on good nutrition and modest but excellence dress sense as both speak volume on one's health and personality. However, that cannot be all that there is to the single life you have to live on earth. Little wonder, kingdom exploits, astounding result, unusual feat has bid us goodbye because our belly has become our God. We have been reduced to Esau who can let go of literally anything to satisfy his taste bud.

"And Esau said, behold, I am at the point to die: and what profit shall my birthright do to me" Gen. 25:32

Esau traded his destiny to satisfy a hunger that is momentary (I wished he never hunger again after the meal). In the same vein, you will be surprised that many young ladies lost their virginity to a date that is not worth more than #5000, a birthday present that is barely #2000 and many more trivial things. Wearing GUCI, Versace, expensive textile and parading eateries perpetually is what many refer to as living and enjoying life at its peak. These wrong ideologies are a clear indication we have not only missed the mark but have also lost touch with one of the master's submission about life.

"Man shall not live by bread alone……"Matt. 4:4

No one who lived by bread alone ever become a living wonder. As long as we continue to navigate life from this misconception we will neither make most nor touch the essence of life.

- **Life is not all about You**

This is one prevalent reason why many are selfish, greedy and careless about how they live. To them whatever life has to offer, decisions they make etc. is all about them or ends with them. This is another great misconception. God's dealing can only begin with you but it is not permitted to terminate with you as a result you are not to intimate others with what your natural advantages, opportunities or whatever you have received of the lord. Anything that stem out of God to men is like a flowing river and must be kept as such don't attempt to convert it to a dam (restrict the flow) as God reach out to men through men.

Also, the earlier we come to term with the fact that individuals are holding the lifeline of a generation (*the salvation or woe that will befall those coming behind is dependent on the quality of our life*) and be taught the networking architecture of life the better. Consciously or unconsciously posterity will be at the mercy of how carefully and carelessly you lived your life. Hitherto, everyone born of woman is caught up in the web of first Adam disobedience without having to partake of the fruit that is the same way you can also decide the fate of a generation. Far from it that the configuration of life is all about you. Hence, one of the greatest mistakes of life is to live for yourself alone.

Fortified with relevant knowledge, it will help us tread with caution and care thereby living with deliberate intention and transgenerational view. Pay the necessary price to reduce the journey of the ones coming behind. Remember, generations will forever drink from the well of wisdom, impact you dug or otherwise be hunted by the pain you left before your exit.

"A good man leaveth an inheritance to his children's children....."

Prov. 13:22

What then is Life?

Life is an errand by the father. He created, designed and wired us uniquely and sends us to earth to deliver a message (answer or solution) to a generation. Consider a DHL courier adequately equipped by the company to deliver a merchandise to a particular receiver any delivery contrary will not be acknowledged nor commended, this is the same prototype with all being (it is noteworthy that the errand is different from person to person). Hence, every mortal on earth are on divine assignment. If this is the accurate definition of life it only means you are alive when you are at the centre of God's purpose and errand for your life.

Interestingly, I have seen many obituary posters with caption *"a life well spent"* until we find out the divine parameters that validate such claim that very submission borne out of perception and philosophy will forever remain untrue. Many will find out in the great beyond they had only breathe oxygen on earth but never lived because they never ran the errand sent them.

Running Divine Errand

If running divine errand is what defines life it must not be subject to guess work or probability meaning it must be a persuaded discovery. All the nitty-gritty about the errand must be consciously and absolutely uncovered by individual. It is quite risky if the narrative is otherwise

"I therefore so run, not as uncertainly; so fight I, not as one that beateth the air" 1 Cor. 9:26

It is practically impossible to run an errand you are clueless about. In view of this, everyone will forever need God in the course of their life. Little wonder the scriptures admonish us in John 15:5 *"I am the vine, ye are the branches: he that abideth in me, and i in him, the same bringeth forth much fruit:* ***for without***

me ye can do nothing". If you have seen people unusually obsessed about God it has nothing to do with religiosity it is on the account of their discovery that the reference for life is drawn from Him alone. Michael W. Smith in one of the lines of his song helplessly declared *"I look to you for life"*.

Jesus the master couldn't live an isolated life from the father throughout the day of His flesh as a deviation no matter how little can jeopardize His assignment. God ordains the blueprint of our life and as a result running divine errand will be in view to the degree to which we align to our pre-ordained destinies by Him.

Finally, as water is the natural habitat of fish any attempt to isolate fish from water is a threat to the life of the fish. In the same vein, God must be the natural habitat of all men you are considered as living when you hang around Him. You must be adequately and continuously instructed if you will ever run divine errand successfully this can only happen when He becomes our natural habitat.

CHAPTER TWO

THE BREVITY OF LIFE

Man who is born of a woman is of few days and full of trouble. Job 14:1

The Good news rendition of Psa. 90:12 reads thus

"Teach us how short our life is, so that we may become wise"

Considering these two scriptures, you will see the "brevity of human life" meaning that our days are numbered in the land of the living. That is, it is a regulated and limited life. Oftentimes the scripture compares our lives to that of a plant which blossom in the morning and wither on exposure to sun in the noon time

Permit me to say, like airtime on the phone, you know how much you have there, so

1. It determines how long your conversations will be while talking to someone via the phone

2. It also determines the kind of people you call. There are some of your contacts that you will need more volume of airtime before you put a call to them

3. With your level of airtime, you call some people, to some you send text message, and to some, you only send a flash.

All these put in our minds that our days here a limited, so as you add more years, be making moves closer to purpose fulfillment and less or no frivolities at all.

Someone who has a 2 year visa to America, won't get there and apply for a contract job that pays salaries every 5 years...

Hence, a man or a woman who is applying his/heart to the wisdom of numbered days

- Cannot be careless with his/her time
- Cannot afford to go everywhere
- Cannot do what others do
- Cannot live his life at the mercy of guess or uncertainty
- Cannot chart the course of life without purpose

By the agency of the spirit of God locate your place in destiny and begin living it with a sense of urgency since you do not have all the time to yourself. If God has not engrace you for a thing, you will struggle there, and while struggling you are wasting the limited time: which is a minus from your regulated life.

We need the grace of God to help us recognise what to do, and doing them promptly and to the best of our capacity. Because you know if a man is timed to be a professional footballer for instance, and he delayed till he clocked 40years old, no matter how spiritual he is that dream is gone. Ability to discern the times and seasons, their essence, and going full length is what determines the real value of life.

CHAPTER THREE

NOW THAT YOU'RE YOUNG

Text: 1John 2:12-17

Youthful age is a age of strength and effective work. It is indeed a developmental age, when all muscles, nerves and hormones in the body develop to maturity. It's why youths wonder about some changes and new developments in their body. Likewise, youthful age is the stage when permanence is being formed in man (both men and women). It is also the stage of life characterized with peak of diverse temptations and deceptions. All these facts about youthful age, makes it most delicate stage in life, which must be guarded with care. Nowadays, most youth don't have knowledge of the age they are, it's why they are found in unlawful and shameful acts all over the world. The devil deceives them with glittery aspect of pleasure and sin, but hides the sting in it away from them.

Now that you're young, there are peculiar knowledge you need to have if you won't regret your privilege to be young in time and eternity. You need to quickly and elaborately understand the peculiarity, criticality and transient nature of youthful age. You need to be equipped on how to adequately handle the pleasures and exuberances that goes along with this particular stage of life. And most importantly, you need to know how to effectively engage your youthful stage of life to guaranty utmost maximization.

Particularly in this teaching, I will carefully x-ray how you're to effectively engage your youthful age. I mean things you should practically achieve in your youth to forestall regret in your adulthood. May the Lord grant you illumination as we study. Amen.

1. **Strength:** Though youthful age is a stage characterized with strength. It is the stage when all nerves, muscles and energies seek for utmost expression (see Proverbs 20:29). Yet, it's a stage to be strong (see 1John2:14b). It's when you should muster all the strength you need for your journey. It's time to be strong spiritually, academically, professionally, ministerially, mentally, emotionally, financially, socially, relationally…. The youthful age is when you're to gather enough strength in all the above mentioned areas; if you won't

end up as a weak and feeble adult. Adequately mustering strength in the above areas guarantees you a holistic adult life in the future. Instead of some youths to focus on mustering strength in the mentioned areas, they encumber themselves in gathering strength, skills and efficiency in lusting after, tricking and luring sexual partners. They daily become strong in immorality and sexual perversions. If you're guilty of this, repent today and turn a new leaf.

2. **Filling yourself with the Word:** The time of youth is a period to carefully, deliberately and adequately fill up your life with the word of God (see 1John2:14c). It is the time to regularly study, meditate on and maximally digest the word of God. The word is to be stored up in your heart and not in your head. The word stored in the head can't help you at the hour of temptation and trials. Only the word in the heart can. The word of God is the only potent antivirus that when properly installed in the heart, prevents sin (see Psalms 119:11). You therefore need to deliberately store it in your heart through Spirit guided study and meditation. The word I am talking about is both Jesus

Christ and Bible Truths (see John 1:1-4). Stop filling your heart with godless, immoral and worldly things, fill your heart with the word; so, you might have victory over sin and self.

3. **Victory over the Wicked One:** The time of youth is a period of evident spiritual battles. The wicked one – Satan, understand that youthful age is when permanence (whether good or bad) is being formed in every human life. Hence, he strategically targets that period to contribute a permanent damage to people's life. It's why he daily throws the fiery darts of temptations, seductions, trials and challenges at you. He wants to size you down. But you need to know that the time of youth is when you're to evidently overcome the wicked one (see 1John 2:13b,14d). It is time to gain victory over self, sin and worldliness. It's time to know and rely solely on the victory Jesus had on the devil on the cross of Calvary. If you refuse to overcome the devil and his antics on your life '***now that you're young***', you might be his slave for the rest of your life in this side of life and eternity. Any sin you fail to overcome in your youth may be your master for the rest of your journey. May the

Lord help you to rise into victory, leaning on the victory of Christ.

4. **Time to Hate the World and All it Offers:** Now that you're young is when to deliberately and eternally hate the world and all it offers (see 1John 2:15-17). As a vibrant Christian youth, you're to love righteousness and hate lawlessness (see Hebrews 1:9). At salvation, God installs eternal hatred for the devil and all his worldly allures in the hearts of all His children (see Genesis 3:15). Sequel to this, you should sternly hate the world and all that is in it. If you love the world, then you hate God. The Bible says if anyone loves the world, the love of the Father – God is not in him/her.

Conclusion

I therefore challenge you to sincerely ruminate on the above discussed issues. Particularly at the period that the whole world celebrate love, you need to x-ray your life in the light of this truth. Have you been adequately, faithfully and holistically engaging your youthful age in things that matters and guaranty your eternity? Have you gained victory over the wicked one? Do you still love or hate the world and all it offers? Carefully and sincerely search your heart. Raise a sincere cry to God in repentance now before it is too late. May you not regret your youthful decisions in Jesus name. Amen.

CHAPTER FOUR

THE BLESSING

Gen 1:28: ***And God blessed them, and God said unto them, be fruitful, and multiply and replenish the earth and subdue it: and have dominion over the fish of the sea, and over the fowl of the air and over every living thing that moveth upon the earth.***

Blessings are words, gifts, provisions, benefits and help needed in the journey of a man. A blessing is a force that makes situations favourable for a man and even his generation. It is sanctions and support that men, group of people or family receive for achievement and purpose fulfillment. It brings great ease to them and makes assignments possible. Blessing is the opposite of curse. The blessing determines the future of a man and it even reverses curses. Blessing is a powerful force to reckon with as it separates men from men. The so called smallest form of blessing should not be overlooked as blessings also has a way of determining the course and results of a man's life.

CHARACTERISTICS OF GOD'S BLESSINGS

The blessing God released upon man in Genesis 1:28

1. **Words**: Blessings most times comes first through words. ***And God blessed them, and God said unto them*……..**Hence, we should be sensitive to words that come from men towards us. Especially when these men have authority over us or even after we have done something that provokes a blessing. Let's note that words of blessings are not to be joked with. Just as we don't take negative words with levity but cancel them immediately, we should also take words of blessings very serious and accept, receive them immediately by saying Amen or words of acceptance such as I receive it. John 6:63. Jesus said, the words that I speak unto you, they are spirit and they are life. Words from God spoken to us activate great things for us when needed. God released a conditional blessing to Isaac in Gen 26:2-4 and it began to manifest in verses 13 and 14 so much that a whole nation envied Isaac and had to send him away. And in verse 26, the same Abimelech who sent him away returned to beg him for a peace mission/covenant. Blessings of God are very powerful and works wonders. Hen God blesses you, take it with all seriousness. When men of God, parents, teachers, elderly ones, friends and even

someone you have helped bless you, receive them with joy. Those blessings, though in words will still manifest physically.

2. **Leads to fruitfulness**: Blessings make men fruitful. One of the ways a curse manifests is fruitlessness. In Mark 11:14 Jesus cursed a fig tree and it dried from it roots. He said, no man eat from thee hereafter forever. This meant the tree would no longer produce fruits for eating. Obviously, fruitfulness is a blessing. ***Ps 128:1-6…***Verse 1 started with the blessing***…blessed is the man that fears the Lord, that walketh in his ways.*** The blessing continued in verse 2 ***…for thou shall eat the labour of thy hands, happy shall thou be and it shall be well with thee,*** verse 3.. ***thy wife shall be as a fruitful vine by the sides of thy house, thy children shall be as olive plants round about thy table***. Obviously, blessings lead to fruitfulness. Have you being struggling to be fruitful, then get the blessing and you will be fruitful. Hannah prayed in Shiloh with all her heart in 1Samuel 1:9-13 and in verse 17, God used Eli to release a blessing to her and she became fruitful. Blessings lead to fruitfulness.

3. **Leads to multiplication**: Not only will blessing lead to increase, it will actually lead to multiplied increase. A blessed man will not only increase once but the increase will be multiplied. ***Gen 26: 12-13. Then Isaac sowed in the land and received in the same year, a hundred fold an hundred fold: and the Lord blessed him. And the man waxed great, and went forward and grew until he became very great.*** Isaac not only increased here, he also multiplied. He did not stop at reaping a hundred fold of seed sown, but he multiplied and became great, multiplied much more till he became very great. That is the essence of blessing. It keeps flowing. Blessing is a spiritual release that keeps working as long as you are connected to the source of blessing.

4. **Leads to replenishment**: This means to restore or to fill up again. Replenishment leads to renewal. When there is replenishment, there won't be lack. A business man who sells goods and always replenish them with new ones will not run out of stock. God's blessings lead to replenishment. Meaning that even after we give out and be a blessing to others, we still receive refreshing, restoration and continue to blossom. God's blessings

won't run out of stock as long as we obey him and we remain connected to him. He is the source that never dries up. When God replenishes us, we don't run out of stock, rather, we keep flourishing. God's replenishment creates a refreshing. God doesn't leave us dry and thirsty, rather he refreshes us daily. Ps 68:19 says ***Blessed be the Lord who daily loads us with benefits***… that is replenishment. In case we spent out what we received yesterday, he comes back in the morning to give us more in loads. Replenishment is blessing indeed. A minister who is not replenished will run out of messages….all he needs is to be restored and reconnected to God and again the blessings will begin to flow. Our God can never run dry; he will continue to replenish us as long as we are daily connected to him.

5. **Leads to dominion**: A blessed man will have dominion. One of the ways to have dominion in a nation is via blessing. This was the fear of the Egyptians when they realized how the Israelites multiplied. They realized that they could outnumber them and use it against them. There is dominion in blessing. Not only does political dominion rule a nation, economic dominion is a powerful

blessing. The ones with economic dominion decide how the political dominion runs their government, because if they withdraw their supplies, that nation suffers. Dominion can also be spiritual. The heart of a king is in the hands of God, so no matter the level of dominion, spiritual dominion can affect both economic and political dominion. Whether physical, spiritual, economical or political, blessing of God gives dominion. The blessing of God made Joseph to have economic dominion, the blessing of God gave David political dominion, the blessing of God gave Elijah spiritual dominion, the blessing of God gave Esau financial and Physical dominion. A blessed man will not be subdued but will rather dominate.

TYPES OF BLESSINGS

People can group blessings in different ways but for the purpose of this study, it would be grouped into conditional or unconditional.

A. **Unconditional blessings:** The general ones are often unconditional and most people can access them. ***Matt 5:45. for he maketh his sun to rise on the evil and on the good and sends rain on the just and the unjust.*** Everyone can breathe in the air that God has provided, that unconditional. So far, you are a human being, wicked or not wicked, air is available to breathe in. The sun shines on you, the rain refreshes the ground and weather for your sake

But there is a greater level than the general.

B.* 1st Level Conditional blessings**: These ones are special blessings meant for Gods children. Unless you are adopted, u might not be able to enjoy the full blessings of a Father to a son. ***Eph 1:3: Blessed be God and Father of our Lord Jesus Christ, who hath blessed us with all spiritual blessings in heavenly places in Christ. These special blessings are for children of God who walk in his ways. There are different promises and blessings of God for children of God. These flows into our lives seemlessly because God is our Father. Anyone who doesn't have God as his father can enjoy the general ones but not the more serious ones. Divine favor, divine protection, divine help, divine opportunities etc work for God's children. Even curses are removed and turned to blessings in the lives of God's children. What about you? Are you his child? If not, give your life to Jesus today. Repent of your sins and ask him to forgive you your sins and accept him as your personal Lord and saviour.

C.* 2nd Level Conditional blessings:* After we become children of God, it is important that we walk with him and obey him. Certain activities key us into covenant blessings of God even as children of God. Abraham, a friend of God was already blessed of God as he was financially blessed, he had dominion, he was fruitful (he had Ishmael and Isaac) etc, yet he couldn't access some height of blessings until his obedience became total. ***Gen 22:16-18 and said, by myself have I sworn, saith the LORD, for because thou hast done this thing and has not withheld thy son, thy only son, that in blessing I will bless you, and in multiplying, I will multiply your seeds as the stars of the heaven and as the sand which is upon the seashore; and thy seed shall possess the gate of his enemies, and in thy seed shall all nations of the earth be blessed; because thou has obeyed my voice*.** Obedience links us to some generational covenanted blessings that we cannot fathom in our minds as children of God. God cherishes obedience. Samuel told Saul, ***behold, to obey is better than sacrifice and to hearken than***

fats of rams. As much as we are children of God, let's endeavor to walk in obedience as this makes God pleased and happy with us and obedience helps us to access higher levels of blessings.

CHAPTER FIVE

TEACH US TO NUMBER OUR DAYS

"So therefore teach us to number our days that we may apply our heart unto wisdom" Psalm 90:12

The Psalmist has perpetually experienced the uncommon mentorship of the lord especially in the matter of wars and this has always culminated in flawless victory. David prevailed in every battle he fought in the day of his flesh even in occasion when he was outnumbered and victory was not in view. He cannot but acknowledge in *Ps. 144:1* that his astounding victories were predicated on the teachings he received from the lord. It is on the strength of this testimony and many others he raised a lamentation of help regarding matter of navigating life and instructions for correct living lest he squanders his days.

There is something about our lives that even the finest and the best of men on earth cannot number nor plot a graph of how it is lived unless we bank on the wisdom of the one who ordains the life in the first place. Life is an eternal trust that no immortal can accurately live until we take advantage of the ancient wisdom before the world began. Hence, living by any other instructions for life other than the ones from the originator of life will spell doom for us all. God by his unsearchable wisdom number the stars in the various galaxies; as plenteous as the strand of hair on human head is, they were all adequately numbered by Him. In view of this our life will only count on earth to the degree to which He mentors us on how to number our days, attempting to navigate life by ourselves will be tantamount to a wasted life.

Unfortunately, culture and tradition of men by intelligence foreign to God's counsel has designed a template and brilliant blueprint of how to live life and it has commanded unimaginable allegiance by the sons of men. This is largely responsible for the reason why many may not step into their ordination nor identify with the purpose of their existence throughout their sojourn on earth. The earlier we break away from this alien instructor and begin to wholly trust Yahweh for instructions on how to number our days our lives will be characterized with nothing but eternal regret, incessant pain, unaccomplished mission, waste etc. If we are ever interested in making our life count as well being a proof producer before departing this realm of life, the prayer of the psalmist must become our obsession. Below are few ancient and patriarchal instructions for life from Yahweh which must be embraced by everyone who desires celestial celebration in the after life.

GODLY WISDOM FOR LIVING

1. **Wisdom of remembering your creator:** God is not an option in the equation of man's journey on earth as many wrongly presume. We owe Him our utmost allegiance all our life and at no point should we be isolated from his apron. Solomon by the agency of God's wisdom submit to us one tested and proven way to number our days in Eccl 12:1a. *"Remember now thy creator in the days of your youth, while the evil days come not".* Our relationship with God is significant to making most of our life and this must happen at the early part of our lives. The youthful days is characterized with vigour and vitality. However, cosmos in her wisdom has also packaged before us vain glory and stimulate our heart with its pursuit so that everyone will be on their toes seeking what the bible call "addition". This is to the end that we might remember

our creator later in life (when we are weak and literally useless) if we ever remembered Him at all.

Also, there is every likelihood that a man forgets God (Jeshurun, Deut 32:15) in the midst of affluence and abundance. One may enter some level of greatness and be completely blinded by influence and reputation that God become inconsequential. It was out of this tendency the Lord gave an eternal ordinance in Deut 8:18. *"But thou shalt remember the LORD thy God: for it is He that giveth thee power to get wealth; that He may establish his covenant which he sware unto thy fathers as it is this day."*

2. **Wisdom of Discipline:** Discipline is a cardinal pillar on which an enviable life suspends. It must be keenly embraced and pursued with intense passion as living a worthwhile life depends on it. Living life without discipline makes one vulnerable and exposed. *"A person without self-control is as defenseless as a city with broken down walls."[NLT] Prov. 25:28*

Demands of discipline

- It takes discipline to be responsible Christian
- It takes discipline to stand out among crowd

- It takes discipline to be sexually pure
- It takes discipline to be achieve success
- It takes discipline to fulfill destiny
- It takes discipline to rise and stay rise

3. **Wisdom of Association:** You are a reflection of your company and close association. A popular author once said your life is at the mercy of the books you read and the friends you keep. No one is likely going to be different from his/her circle of association. Hence, the bible emphatically advocates wisdom and caution when it comes to identifying with one.

   "As in water face answereth to face,……." Prov. 27:19

4. **Wisdom of living with eternity in view:** you do not have all the time to yourself on earth everyone will surely breath their last in due time. Interestingly, everyday of your life is a step closer to the grave. There is realm of existence yonder where all flesh will stand before the maker to give account of their deeds in the flesh good or evil accompanied with commensurate rewards. Living with this mindset will condition you to live with caution here on

earth and accountability consciousness when death closes your eye.

Maximizing Birthday

Norm and tradition of men has taught us to throw feast, paint the town red, litter the media with the finest of pictures on this notable day (which is not bad in themselves). While it is obviously a day of massive joy and celebration it is also important to note that it is a day of personal solemn assembly and sober reflection. However, the narrative is people choose to be lost in the ecstasy and euphoria of the excitement and bother less about the latter. There is obviously more to birthday than partying and feasting and to many that is one of their days of negligence and compromise borne of the ecstatic moment. It is interesting to know that birthday a supposed reminder of the day you are born is also a reminder of death day (in case you have forgotten that you are a pilgrim and life is ephemeral). It doesn't cease to amaze me how many have become obsessed with material possession, bent on catching fun all their life, living life with ardent mindset that they are going to be trapped in here for life. If you like, live long like Methuselah, it has been ordained for every man to transit to the afterlife either by naturality or by raptulity. It is in the afterlife we shall come to term with the fact that material things are really immaterial and many things that commanded our attention the most are inconsequential. Hence, the need to review our priorities lest we amount to waste in the days of our flesh.

"While we look not at the things which are seen, but at the things which are not seen: for things which are seen are temporal; but the things which are not seen are eternal" 2 Cor. 4:18

How to maximize birthday celebration

i. Thank God for life

   "A living dog is better than a dead lion" according to the scripture. You owe your existence hitherto to God alone. Don't be casual with the gratitude it must be borne out of deep meditation and thankful heart.

ii. Recount God's faithfulness

   Go back to the memory lane and consider his faithfulness in your from ages past till present. You will be humbled to find out how innumerable mercies of the lord you have received. Don't trivialize it

iii. Reflect on the journey so far

"The secret to the future is in the past" Mike Murduck

Take time and hold a meeting with your tripartite (body, soul and spirit) nature all in attendance. Be deliberate and intentional about it. Learn from both the strength and weakness of the past. Refuse to be hunted by the errors or mistakes behind rather garrison your heart and prepare for the journey that lies ahead

iv. Meditate on your destiny graph

Ask yourself rhetorical questions and sincerely provide an answer:

- Have you discover your purpose or you are still fighting as one beating the air?
- To what degree does your life bear resemblance to the one you are ordained for by God?
- Are you operating steadily in purpose or vice versa?

- Is the graph of your life tending toward the positive or negative axis?
- Are you in the right geographical location?

v. Plan for the future

At the end of the personal court session you must have come up with lots of discoveries and conclusion. Deploy them and confront the future with sense of mission and intentionality.

vi. Make yourself happy

Celebrate yourself personally or in company as the case may be. Do this within your means and always remember that your happiest day can also be the day you are most vulnerable.

Conclusively, as we celebrate this awesome day annually we must not be carried away with the jamboree to neglect the other weightier matter. Do this hence, and watch your life radiate and ooze out meaning and essence; behold I show you a more excellent way.

www.ingramcontent.com/pod-product-compliance
Lightning Source LLC
LaVergne TN
LVHW020527160826
845677LV00015B/3954
9798845622105